Ketogenic Diet For Beginners: Your Guide To Starting Keto, Ketone And Ketogenic Diet Meal Plans

Michael Crow 2017 All Rights Reserved

TABLE OF CONTENTS

INTRODUCTION

Congratulations for purchasing this book

Granted that you might have purchased your diet books on what 7 days or 21-day meal plan for weight loss. However, as interesting as this might sound, your weight loss goals will still be greatly hindered if your knowledge of the diet. To get the best out of your Ketogenic diet, your meal plan must be carefully implemented.

This is what this book has been set out to do. It is mainly to provide you with all the necessary information that will help you to achieve weight loss from the beginning to the end of your diet. Beginners will find this book a useful tool and even those who have experience in the diet will equally find this book a useful tool. You will know through this book how to enter into ketosis quickly for rapid weight loss, how to measure your ketosis, what to eat and what not to eat, ketoacidosis, benefits from being on this diet, shopping tips for your diet food items, how to maintain a low budget Ketogenic diet, advice on maintaining groups that will encourage your weight loss.

I welcome you to this wonderful book that will serve as an indispensable tool for your weight loss.

CHAPTER ONE

The History of Ketogenic

During the middle ages, as childhood epilepsy ravaged the strength of juveniles, a burden squared on the shoulders of parents to find a treatment that will stop the suffering to which kids were subjected to. This epilepsy epidemic stood at that time before many like a consuming fire. It must be understood that medicine as at that stage was still in its infancy compared to now where modern medicine can cure almost every form of the disease that tries to plague the lives of men. As the searching for this cure to childhood epilepsy dragged on, the society as at that period started to rely on alternatives to treat their young. Worn out by the scourge of epilepsy that flogged kids to convulsion, people started relying on an ancient model of treatment – fasting as a means of treating

1

seizures. Fasting as a means of holding down raging epilepsy that was fighting furious wars on the body and the brains of kids won an array of successful medallion like a young athlete upon his debut appearance in sport. This brought hope and joy to the families of many who had sunk deep into the dark tunnel of hopelessness. For them, respite came at last from the insurmountable mountain of convulsion will finally be leveled. The success of this method of treatment gained a higher currency as it was relied upon solely as the means of treating epilepsy in kids in the early 1900's which had hitherto waged savage wars on juveniles at that time.

The Failure of the Early Diet

Though fasting was employed, its efficacy only lasted as long as the fasting continued. Once the fasting is dotted with a pause, epilepsy invaded kids with athletic agility thus rendering fasting only as a yoke that the young of that time must bear to be epilepsy-free. Between the 1900s to the 1920s, modern medicine has to a large extent experienced significant growth that it could be administered to epileptic kids. To what extent were these drugs effective? It was this question that led to the first light of Ketogenic diet to shine forth in 1921. This discovery was shouldered by Doctor Wilder and it was at the John Hopkins Hospital that this discovery was made.

Trouble Times for the Diet

After love affairs with drugs, the society once again found itself drawn by Ketogenic diet, which in the middle ages could be related to fasting. This diet was majorly on fat and it restricted carbohydrates intake. However, a wind of change started to blow against the continued survival of this young and formidable diet. As the wind of change blew harder, the rise of Ketogenic diet was crippled by the disfavor that later saluted it. In the U.S, anti-fat campaigns mounted severe pressure on the weak foundation of Ketogenic diet. Soon, Ketogenic diet found this pressure too much to bear and it crumbled to obscurity. These anti-fat campaigns won the day that they received even the U.S government support. The anti-fat campaign's report was later codified in government reports on dietary because of the McGovern Report. Beyond the anti-fat campaigns which had made nonsense of Ketogenic diet as at that time, there was also a breakthrough in the science of medicine in the 30s, 40s, and 50s which seemed to be a viable means of treatment than Ketogenic diet.

A resurrected form of Ketogenic diet with some few modifications known as Medium Chain

Triglyceride diet found expression, but its usage died as quickly as it came to limelight in 1994.

The True Success Story

As time piled up, the Ketogenic diet was once again able to stage a comeback to the scene with the story of a two-year-old who had had seizures that refused to bow to the control of medications or other forms of treatment including brain surgery. The boy's father hungered by the burning desire to discover more knowledge about the Ketogenic diet started digging up information about the diet. He sought for the information and found it which led to the end of John Hopkins Medical Centre. The boy's seizure was completely controlled as long as he was on the diet. Due to the successful taming of the seizure by the boy's father in administering the diet, he created a foundation which produced many videos, books and sponsored conferences for the training of doctors and diet experts for the implementation of Ketogenic diet. Today, the diet has now become the subject of study in the medical field which is applicable to different types of diseases. Although the Ketogenic diet has gained a lot of acceptance among medical experts, the principal reason for this ton of interest and acceptance is just for one purpose – to find a Ketogenic diet drug.

In the final analysis of this historical discussion, it must be noted that when Ketogenic diet attained the status of media publicity many years ago, so many critics complained that long-term studies on Ketogenic diet have not been carried out. At present, a sea of study has been conducted on the diet and those studies have not established the negative effects of Ketogenic diet. The Ketogenic diet has been called by different names recently. At present, there are so many researches that have been published pointing to the effectiveness of Ketogenic diet has left so much to be desired.

Explaining Ketogenic Diet

If you have followed me very closely, you would have noticed that we have known relatively what Ketogenic Diet is as a result of the explanation supplied in the introduction. However, I want to give you a definition of what Ketogenic diet means. By definition, Ketogenic diet is a low-carb and high-fat diet in which the amount of carb is lowered and the amount of fat taken is increased. The primary purpose of the Ketogenic diet is to encourage your body system to stop burning carbs as fuel and burn fat as ketones. This process is achieved by lowering the level of carb intake to 50 grams in a day. But what is ketosis? Ketosis is a metabolic process where the production of ketones by the liver is undertaken. What usually happens when the intake of carbohydrate is lowered is that the body adjust and shifts into ketosis. A high percentage of cells in the human body utilizes ketones as a source of energy. The usage of ketone bodies by the cells usually occur at a time of long fast or restricted consumption of carbohydrate. Ketones can provide energy for most organs in the body. It is very important to know that glucose is the primary energy for most cells in the body. For the purpose of conserving the use of energy for futuristic use, the body stores excess glucose as glycogen. This glycogen is found in the liver and in the muscle. The glycogen stored in the liver is used to maintain the usual levels of glucose in the blood. In contrast, glycogen that has been stored up are for the purposes of fueling muscle activities. When the intake of carbohydrate restriction is in top gear, protein, as well as fats, can be used as a source of energy. The majority of cells in the body can make use of fatty acids for energy. In a time of shortage or complete lack of carbohydrate, the liver breaks down fat. At such times, ketone bodies can be used by most cells. The production of ketone in excess of what the body requires makes the level of ketones to increase resulting in what is known as ketosis.

What to Know About Ketogenic Diet

When dietary conditions are normal, the human body runs on a combination of the following – carbohydrates, protein, and fat. The moment carbohydrates are eliminated from food that is consumed, the reservoir of carbohydrate in the body are used up. In order to continue working, the body must find an alternative source of energy that it would use as fuel. Among the fuels that the body needs are free fatty acids, which many cells in the body can use. Some cells in the body cannot, however, use Free Fatty Acid. The brain cannot use it. They can make use of ketone bodies. When this free fatty acid is not completely broken down in the liver, ketone bodies are produced. This fatty acid that has not been broken down, will serve as a source of fuel for the brain.

Low Carb Diet

Confusion has arisen that has many people thinking that whenever they are on a diet that is low in carbohydrate, they begin to tell themselves that they are on a Ketogenic diet. This seeming confusion has been compounded by the belief that low carb diet and Ketogenic diet are the same. However, I will explain to you that there is a great difference between these two diets. These differences are as follows:

- The composition of the Diet: This is perhaps is the greatest distinguishable factor between the Ketogenic diet and other diets that are low in carbs. While the Ketogenic diet is majorly a low-carb and high-fat diet, in the case of other forms of diets that are low in carb, it could be low carb and high protein. It is important to know that your fat level in a low carb diet does not matter since the body runs on carbohydrate as its key fuel source. Conversely, in a Ketogenic diet, about 70 percent of your calories per day are from fat, since fat has now become your primary source of fuel.

- Percentage of Carb Intake: This is another form of the difference between Ketogenic diet and other forms of low carb diet. Many types of research have suggested that eating less than 30% of calories gotten from carbohydrate. That is 50 to about 125 grams of carbs daily. On the other hand, on a Ketogenic diet, the intake of carbohydrate is about 5 to 15% per day and a maximum threshold of 50 grams of carbs.

- The ratio of Weight Loss: It will be important for you to know that the weight lost on the Ketogenic diet is faster than those experienced in other low carb diets. This is not a conjecture or manufacture of facts. In

8

our first difference that was explained above, we have stated that in Ketogenic diet, your intake of carbohydrate is lower than it can be in other forms of low carb diets. While in other diets, your carb can be up to 30%, but in Ketogenic diet, the carb intake can be just 10%. Now looking at the above, who will lose weight faster? Certainly, the person who is on a Ketogenic diet.

- Fuel Source: The source of fuel in the body when a person is on a low carb diet is carbohydrate while in the case of Ketogenic diet, the main source of fuel comes from ketone bodies which are mostly fat.

- Activity Stage: It is important to know that during the time of abundance of carbohydrate source in the body system, ketone bodies are normally dormant and inactive. As a matter of fact, they are sleeping and do not wake up. However, during the time of shortage of carb and long fasting periods, ketone bodies play a more active role than any form of fuel source. The brain and other cells that make use of predominantly another source of fuel such as carb will switch and begin to use fat.

Similarities

Even though there are many differences between Ketogenic diet and other low carb diets, it is important to know that there are similarities between these two diets. I will make an attempt to explain just a few to you.

- Purpose: No one ever undertakes a low-carb diet or Ketogenic to add more weight. People engage on low carb diet to lose more weight. This is the similarity between Ketogenic diet and low carb diet which is weight loss as their main goal. This similarity does not, however, change the status of a person who is on a low-carb diet to a ketone diet.

- Carb Consumption: I will also emphatically state here that in both diets, there is a certainly a level of carb consumption. When people decide to engage in low carb diets or Ketogenic diet, they will still have to consume carbohydrate in one form or the other and that is the similarity between the two diets.

- Protein and other Food Sources are consumed: In both diets, there is the intake of protein and other food sources. However, caution is recommended here when consuming protein because when it is high, it may hinder you from entering ketosis. We will discuss that more when we approach the short topic "How to Enter Ketosis Fast."

Starting the Ketogenic Lifestyle

Starting Ketogenic lifestyle at the beginning of your diet requires you to know some important things. It is essential for you to understand that your fuel metabolism changes from carb to fat. Thus, as the river of carb dries up because you have cut it down from your food, your body makes an adjustment to burn an alternative fuel source which is fat, and it is broken down to ketones in the body. Your weight loss goal is achieved when you have fully entered into ketosis. In Ketosis, your body burns fat instead of conventional carb as a fuel source. But what does it take to make the change? Habit formations are one of your greatest aid. You need to develop a good habit that will help you stay in ketosis. While the cravings for carb might come down heavily upon you, you have to fight it off. A heavy loading of carb destroys your weight loss goal. Further down in this book, I will give you a Ketogenic kitchen list. It is good to have those food items in your pantry. Since the Ketogenic diet resolves around a full optimization of ketosis, I will give you some aid that will help you speed up your ketosis.

- **Limit Carb Intake**: One of the easiest and quickest ways to reach ketosis is by restricting carb intake per day to 20% of total calories. However, the higher you reduce the intake of carbs, the better. Some have lowered carb intake to 5% and got better results. To lower carbs, choose the fruits with low carb content and veggies with low carb content. Marinate them with healthy fats.

Your blueberries or raspberries should be soaked in unsweetened coconut milk or heavy cream. And then your green veggies, broccoli, zucchini, and cauliflower should be covered with healthy olive oil or grass-fed butter.

- **Incorporate Coconut Oil in Your diet**: Consuming coconut oil is one quick route to ketosis. Coconut Oil contains fats called medium-chain triglycerides (MCTs). The good thing about MCT is that unlike most fats, MCTs are quickly absorbed and transported straight to the liver, where they are used quickly as converted energy or converted into ketones. Many are of the view that consuming coconut oil is one of the greatest ways to increase ketone levels in the lives of those afflicted with Alzheimer's disease and other nervous system diseases. Coconut oil has four basic types of MCTs. Fifty percent of the coconut oil is fat that is gotten from lauric acid. A higher percentage of lauric acid as suggested by many types of research produces a more sustainable level of ketosis. The reason for this is because it metabolizes slowly than other MCTs. In epileptic kids, MCTs have been used successfully to induce ketosis without limiting the number of carbs as it happens in a normal Ketogenic diet.

- **Practice fasting:** To speed up ketosis, intermittent fasting is a necessity. Fasting is one of the fundamental weapons for getting into quick ketosis. Fasting can also be used to maintain ketosis since you are cutting down on calories and not eating protein or carbohydrate. Before you begin fasting, it is best to lower your carb for some few days before the fasting in order to avoid a hypoglycemic incident. It is easier to maintain ketosis if you are able to fast intermittently. As you undertake your fast, I recommend taking herbal teas and hydrating and taking organic coffee with MCT oil, or grass-fed butter or coconut oil. Ketone production is boosted by the small and medium chain fats, which go a long way in stabilizing blood sugar more effectively than water fasting. Many people have reported excellent feelings while fasting.
- **Increase fat intake**: Eating plenty of healthy fat increases ketone levels and help you reach ketosis. A low carb keto diet not only reduces the level of carbs but very effective for weight loss, metabolic health and optimal exercise performance. When the Ketogenic diet is used for epilepsy treatment, it will be higher in fat percentage of about 85–90% of

calories from fat. It is important to note that an increase in the consumption of fat does not necessarily mean a correspondent increase in ketone levels in the body system. Additionally, since the Ketogenic diet composes of a large percentage of fat, it is good when making the choice of fat to choose those that are high in quality. Such quality fat includes – coconut oil, lard, olive oil, avocado oil, butter, and tallow. Furthermore, high-fat foods that are very healthy yet low in carb content. However, for those whose main goal of engaging in the Ketogenic diet is weight loss, you have to ensure that you are not consuming too many calories in total, as this may prevent your weight loss goals.

- **Obtain A ketone Meter**: The reason why you need a ketone meter to measure your ketosis is so that you know once you have entered ketosis the steps to take. It is important because there are many instruments out there. However, Ketone meters are the most effective and standard form of measuring your ketosis. However, it has one major problem. It is too expensive. A single ketone meter can cost up to $ 100 and the test per strip can be up to five bucks. The content of the meter includes a lancet pen, which is a device that jabs you in order to get blood. The meter beyond testing for ketones in your bloodstream, it also tests for glucose. The two most popular blood ketone meters in the market today – Precision Brand and Nova Max. Both of them can be ordered from amzon.com. The problem with Nova Max as reported by many users is that it frequently gives you an error message and it does not give you any reading below 0.5 although their test strips are cheaper. Though precision strip gives you more accuracy with lesser error messages, it is much expensive per strips than Nova Max. One problem though it is that precision is not too effective on glucose measurement, but it measures ketones very effectively. However, if you want to decide which of the two products that you want to purchase, I will suggest that you read the reviews on amazon. This will help you make your mind up.

CHAPTER TWO

List of Persons Who can go on a Ketogenic Diet?

The ketogenic diet is a diet that almost everybody can go on and lose weight rapidly. However, there are restrictions. The fundamental question is, can Ketogenic diet be undertaken by everybody? Are there people who are supposed to go on a Ketogenic diet or are there people who should not go on a Ketogenic diet? Let me try to make some list here.

- Pregnant and Breastfeeding Mom: Though a pregnant woman can go on a Ketogenic diet, but it must be carefully done with the guidance of a physician or dietitians. There is a risk for a pregnant woman. Serious weight loss at the time of pregnancy may affect the fetus or the baby because of the release of toxins. Weight loss during pregnancy and breastfeeding may have negative consequences for the baby or fetus as a result of the production of toxins by the fat cells. However, there is much research that encourages pregnant and breastfeeding moms to go on a Ketogenic diet.

- Type 1 Diabetes: In the case of type 1 diabetes, the body's defense system which can also be called the immune system assails a part of the body's pancreas. The reason why this happens is not known. The body's immune system erroneously destroys the cells in the pancreas because it sees them as foreign. These cells which are destroyed by the immune system are known as islets and they are the ones that are responsible for dictating the levels of glucose in the blood stream and when they see that the level of glucose is high, they produce the amount of insulin required to bring blood sugar to normal levels. Without insulin, blood sugar can be really high and a lot of devastating consequences can occur. I needed to explain this. Now, this is the catch when you are on a Ketogenic diet, there is a switch in the fuel source. Your body switches from burning carbs stored as glucose to fats. Since the intake of carb is limited, fat is used as a fuel source. Remember that at this stage your body is no longer taking in glucose. It will begin to break down the fat in the muscles and other parts of the body system. This happens when you are on a Ketogenic diet and you have entered ketosis; what you use as energy is fat and it is the breakdown of this fat that results in the buildup of ketone bodies. Ketone bodies enter the blood stream and a chemical imbalance occurs which is known as diabetic ketoacidosis. To engage in the Ketogenic diet without the direction of a physician is dangerous for Type 1 diabetes.

- Children: Kids can go on a Ketogenic Diet. Remember in the chronicle or history of Ketogenic diet we stated that one of the things that made it stage a good come back was when it was successfully administered on a kid to control his epilepsy in the 1990's.
- Elderly: Ketogenic diet is a diet that everyone can go on despite age categorization. It would, however, be advised that before the elderly decide to proceed on a Ketogenic diet, they consult their dietitians or physicians.

Benefits of Ketogenic Diet

We will discuss the benefits that can be obtained once you are on a Ketogenic diet. Once you are on a Ketogenic diet, these are the benefits that you will derive from being on the diet:

- **Epilepsy**: In the chronicles of Ketogenic diet, I have expounded with clarity how in the 1920s, the society heavily relied on a Ketogenic diet as a means of fighting epilepsy. Though drugs were to some extent effectively good, the diet was successfully dealing with epilepsy. It will be recalled that in 1994, the father of a kid who got tired of trying out conventional medicine because the seizure which his kid was having at that point defied any form of treatment. They had tried their hands on modern medicine but failure hit them back at their faces. However, when they finally lay their hands on the Ketogenic diet, the kid was completely healed as long as he was on the diet. Beyond administering this diet on kids in those days, Ketogenic diet has successfully been tested on adults with amazing therapeutic results. Today, Ketogenic diet can handle epilepsy both in the young and adults.

- **Reversing Type 2 Diabetes**: This is one of the benefits of being on a Ketogenic diet. The many success stories of this diet which research has proven are that since the amount of carbohydrate that you take is lowered, then your blood sugar level is brought to the barest minimum. It is important to note that carb stimulates the body system to discharge the hormone called insulin. So when carb intake is lowered, the body does not release more insulin to control the blood sugar which will, in turn, increase the burning of fat that has been stored in the body. How then does this work in reversing Type 2 diabetes? The answer to the question is simple. The fundamental problem faced by people with diabetes is a high amount of blood sugar that comes primarily from carb intake. Once a person in on a Ketogenic diet, since he eats a fewer amount of carbs, the body can easily control the amount of blood sugar which has the capacity of reversing Type 2 diabetes.

- **Weight Loss**: What happens during ketosis? Your body switches from burning carbs as fuel into burning fat which results in tremendous weight loss. As you go deeper into the sea of ketosis, your body burns fat resulting in weight loss. Instead of other types of diets which many have been using for weight loss without success, with Ketogenic diet, you lose body fat and weight quickly.

- **Effective Mental Agility**: When ketosis mode is fully activated, there is a constant supply of ketones to the brain. Remember that when the body is not in ketosis mode and carb is steadily fed into the body system, the brain makes use of carb as a fuel source and many are of the opinion that to increase mental agility and focus, more carbs need to be consumed. On the contrary, when you are fully in ketosis, because your body makes a huge change in fuel consumption, meaning it burns more fat rather than the conventional carbs, fat in your body are broken down into ketone bodies. Other organs in the body can make use of fat, however, the brain makes use of ketones broken down from fat. During ketosis, there is usually increased the flow of ketone bodies to the brain giving it effective mental agility and focus.

- **Acne Reduction**: It is has been reported with huge success that many people who have acne problems when on low carb diet like the Ketogenic diet that acne is drastically reduced. When on a Ketogenic diet, the intake of carb is lowered. Where carbs are taken, the body needs to produce the hormone called insulin to reduce the amount of blood sugar in the blood stream. Acne is mostly caused and driven by insulin. It is the cornerstone of acne. Besides acting as the main agent that motivate skin cells to manufacture sebum (an oily secretion secreted by the sebaceous gland that lubricates the hair and skin that gives protection against bacteria) and keratin (a fibrous insoluble protein that is the main structural element in hair and nail), it heightens the secretion of many other hormones that causes acne. What does this all mean? When you are on a low carb diet like Ketogenic diet, the secretion of insulin to lower the amount of blood sugar in your blood stream is not necessarily needed since your body as a fat burning machine, does not need that. Insulin, being one of the fathers of acne, will be curtailed since you do not take many carbs that will summon its presence in your blood stream. When there is no sugar to reduce in the blood, I bet that insulin will continue sleeping.

- **Enhanced Stamina**: During the Ketogenic diet, your physical stamina and endurance will be enhanced since you will have access to storage of fat that your body has reserved. At a time of intense exercise, your stored carbs will melt away like the dissolving ice beaten by summer light within a couple of hours. On the other hand, your fat storage can last longer than your carbs. When you are carb adapted, your fat stores are easily depleted during a short time of intense exercise and to refill, you must keep eating. However, when you are on a Ketogenic diet, most of the fuel that is available is fat with long lasting effects than your regular carb stores. The body and your brain are energized by your fat stores making you last longer in exercise and have a lot of stamina than someone who is relying on carbs for his stamina and endurance.

- **Enhanced Performance**: Since your body is experiencing a shift from what it is used to, it is possible that at the formative stage of the Ketogenic diet, you might experience some form of reduced performance. But will this remain for a long time? Certainly no. The benefits of going Ketogenic are more long term than short term. Today, there are many athletes that are going Ketogenic and have seen very effective and great performances especially in long distance running. As I have explained earlier, your fat stores last longer than your carb stores. Since fat stores last longer, an athlete can perform for a prolonged period without refueling with external energy.

- **Decreased Aging**: With Ketogenic diet, your body can maintain a very nice look. When you have entered ketosis, ketone bones are produced. These bodies may decrease the aging process by blocking a group of enzymes known as Histone Deacetylases. The enzymes function to keep a couple of genes known as Forkhead box O3 and Metallothionein 2A turned off. These genes can empower other cells to resist oxidative stress. The good thing is that the ketone bodies produce when a full fledge ketosis has been entered can block Forkhead box O3 allowing the genes to be reactivated which prevents oxidative stress because it is this oxidative stress that indirectly causes aging. Besides, the Ketogenic diet reduces blood sugar levels. It is important to know that when sugar levels are reduced, glycation and the production of enhanced glycation by-product materials made from high blood sugar heightens tissue damage, diabetes, and aging. Finally, Ketogenic diet is a catalyst that reduces triglycerides which are known for causing a lot of terminal diseases.

- **Alzheimer disease**: This is a mental disorder that causes dementia because of the progressive degradation of the brain. One of the features of this disease is a decreasing ability of the brain to metabolize glucose.

Whenever the brain is unable to metabolize glucose, it can have a lot of impact on the brain. However, with ketone bodies when a person is fully into ketosis, the supply of ketones to the brain when on a Ketogenic diet reduces the brain over dependence on glucose.

How to Measure Ketosis

- **Urine Test**: This is one way to measure your ketones for the purpose of ascertaining whether you are in ketosis. Using urine strips, you can easily and simply determine your ketosis without much cost. Testing your urine will readily reveal to you if you have gone over the rooftop by eating higher than recommended carbs. Once you dip the stick into your urine, it will turn purple indicating the presence of ketones in your body. A good result for the presence of ketones is dark purple color. When no precise color is shown, it means that you might not have entered ketosis yet.
- **Obtain a ketone Meter**: Ketone meters are the most effective and standard form of measuring your ketosis. However, it has one major problem. It is too expensive. A single ketone meter can cost up to $ 100 and the test per strip can be up to five bucks. The content of the meter includes a lancet pen, which is a

device that jabs you in order to get blood. The meter beyond testing for ketones in your bloodstream, it also tests for glucose. The two most popular blood ketone meters in the market today – Precision Brand and Nova Max. Both of them can be ordered from amazon.com. The problem with Nova Max as reported by many users is that it frequently gives you an error message and it does not give you any reading below 0.5 although their test strips are cheaper. Though precision strip gives you more accuracy with lesser error messages, it much expensive per strips than Nova Max. One problem though it is that precision is not too effective on glucose measurement but it measures ketones very effectively. However, if you want to decide which of the two products that you want to purchase, I will suggest that you read the reviews on amazon. This will help you make your mind up.

- **Ketone Breath Analysers**: Measuring your breath through the breath ketone analyzers is a good way of knowing whether you have fully entered into ketosis. They are very expensive and they can be ordered from Amazon. However, they are less expensive than the blood ketone meters. They come in two forms – disposable and reusable. The results of these tests come in different form. They will not give you an accurate result of what the level of your blood ketones is but rather display for you an array of colors. It is not a form of yes or no. It will either give this color for positive that you are in ketosis or that color for negative that you are not in ketosis. All the same, when you measure your blood ketones with ketone breath analyzers, the yellow and tan are indicators that the result is negative that you have not yet entered ketosis. When the result shows you pink or purple, it means that you are fully into ketosis. One major problem as complained by users of these breath analyzers is their inaccuracy. Sometimes, the results obtained are not true. Besides that, I will not encourage anyone who is just starting a Ketogenic diet to use the breath analyzers. Blood ketone meters are by far the best since they give you a much accurate result. If you are a seasoned dieter on Ketone, you can try this breath analyzer since the chances are that you are following your diet right. You know what you want. However, for beginners, it is good to use the blood ketone meters. Besides, the instructions for usage on the disposable has been reported to be complex, and unless carefully used, mistakes abound.

How to Know When You Have Entered Ketosis

The fundamental goal of being on a Ketogenic diet is to enter ketosis in which case your body makes a huge switch from a carb burning machine into a fat burning machine and that is actually where the weight loss begins. How do you know that you have entered ketosis for your Ketogenic diet to be effective? How do you know that you are fully into ketosis for an optimum weight loss which is the basis for being on the diet? There are many of those signs and I will explain them here.

Excessive thirst and sometimes feeling dry in the mouth. When you feel that, it might be possible that you have fully activated the ketosis mode. To resolve this, it is important for you to take a lot of liquids such as water and salt so that you can obtain a lot of electrolytes.

Frequent urination. Ketone bodies are produced when you are fully into ketosis. One of the ketones that are produced is called acetoacetate, whose end is in your urine. For most beginners on the Ketogenic diet, it is possible to experience frequent visits to the bathroom. Do not be alarmed, it could be that you have entered ketosis.

28

The low rate of hunger. This is the evidence of many people who are on a Ketogenic diet. The reason for this is diverse. When you are in ketosis, your body uses its fat stores for fuel. Again, due to a high fraction of protein and vegetable intake and the changes experienced by your hunger hormones could cause that. Additionally, when the urge for eating does not come more frequently, the possibility is that you are in ketosis.

Your breath is another fundamental index for dictating that you are in ketosis. As you entered ketosis, it is possible that your breath takes on a fruity texture. The reason for this is because of ketone bodies being passed through your breath. The particular ketone that is responsible for that is called acetone. To solve this issue, it is advisable to brush your teeth as many times a day that you can afford to do. If that is what you are currently experiencing, then I congratulate you because it is possible that you have entered ketosis. However, this bad breath is transient and not permanent. As your time in the diet enlarges, the fruity breath goes away on its own.

Rapid weight loss. To lose weight rapidly, then Ketogenic diet is your solution. And that is one of the things you will experience once you have entered ketosis. Most people undergo rapid weight loss in their first week of dieting this is because a lot of your fat stores is being used plus carbs and water in your body system are being utilized by your body system.

Energetic strength. The level of energy you feel in your body will increase. Your fat stores are being used up during this process and fat in your body is readily broken down. Before this stage is attained, at the early stages of dieting, it is possible to have a Keto flu. This is because your body at that period is working very hard to adjust to the new fuel source. Some people feel tiredness, feeling sick and other types of feelings. As you age in the diet, all of these feelings will disappear. You will begin to feel strengthened and energetic.

Increased presence of ketones in the blood. As your blood sugar levels reduce, something else fills your blood stream – ketones. When you gather more distance in the diet, you will be burning mainly fat and ketones as your fuel source.

Improved mental focus. At the start of the Ketogenic diet, your body makes an adaptation from burning carbs to burning fat. When you entered into ketosis, your brain begins to burn ketones instead of glucose gotten from carbs. So when you begin to experience improved mental focus, it is one of the indexes of ketosis.

Tiredness and exhaustion. When making a switch from carbs to Ketogenic diet, many dieters face a lot of issues. At the early phase of dieting, many feel tired and exhausted. This is because of the initial change in the fuel source. However, if endured, the long-term benefits of Ketogenic are more than the reactions that your body feels. When you begin to feel that, it is possible that you have entered ketosis.

Digestion during the beginning period of the dieting on a Ketogenic diet may be a problem. Depending on your body system, this is not common to everyone. Some experience constipation. This is however limited to the transitional phase of the diet. The moment you are fully transitioned, this will stop. This may also be an indication of ketosis. As I said people's experience on the Ketogenic diet varies. Yours might not be the same with that of another.

Sleeplessness is another index that ketosis has been entered. This experience is usually for those who first start out on the diet. A change of diet for some has been associated with insomnia. Nevertheless, this does not last for long as it soon disappears within a short time.

CHAPTER THREE

What to Eat During Ketogenic Diet

Planning is very important for every Ketogenic diet that you decide to go on because the diet works on recognized principles without the observance of which, quick weight loss might not be attained. The amount of food you eat, the type of food you eat will either delay your ketosis or hinder it completely. The less quantity of carbs you eat, let us say 18 to 20 grams daily, the better your chances of getting into ketosis and if you decided to narrow it down to 15 grams, the better your chances of entering into the state of ketosis within a short time. The recommended intake of carbs in a proper Ketogenic diet is within the range of 20 percent to 30 percent. However, to get better results, it is good if you can lower your carb intake. For your nutrients, it is recommended that it should be 70 percent, fats should be 25 percent and your carbs should be 5 percent. Your nutrient intake can also be structured in this form, 70% fats, 25% protein, and 5% carbohydrate. The source of your carbs should be mostly obtained from veggies, dairy products, and nuts. I have listed some nutritious food that you can eat.

- Meat: Here you can eat lamb, beef, pork, etc.
- Eggs: They are very rich in fat content.
- Cheese: Make sure that they do not contain carbs
- Veggies: They contain some amount of carbs but make sure that what you eat is not too rich in carbs, vegetables like cabbage and lettuce are okay.
- Nuts: They are a good source of low carbs especially walnut and almonds.

However, always eat your nut with a sense of moderation not to blow your carb intake over the top.

What Not to Eat

There are certain food products which you must avoid if you want to have a good result from your Ketogenic diet. The majority of your meal should be protein and vegetables. Never eat starchy carbs like bread, pasta, cereals, potatoes, beans, legumes or some fruits. They will hinder the whole process of your Ketogenic diet and can stop you from getting into ketosis.

Why A Diet Plan?

The Ketogenic diet is built on a strong foundation of healthy foods that help achieve weight loss effortlessly. If you carefully prepare a meal plan, it will prevent you from ordering takeout. This diet will then culture you into a habit that will eliminate completely the desire for processed foods which will, in turn, help you to lead the healthy life and attain weight loss without a struggle.

Knowledge is information and others called it power. And that is true. If you look at some of the shopping list mentioned in this book, you will notice that it will help you to become an informed shopper who knows the healthy foods to buy that will give him the best result in eating foods which will help your Ketogenic diet. When you shop by yourself, the shopping educates you in buying food items that are necessary for your ketone diet which will, in the end, give you healthy appearance and make your weight loss aim a reality.

He who fails to plan they say plans to fail. Having a meal plan will save you a lot of money. In this book, we have covered the low dollar Ketogenic diet and how it will help you to cut down on the cost of your Ketogenic diet. If you plan well, the meal plan will let you know what you need to purchase which will, in the long run, reduce cost.

If you want to lead the Ketogenic diet life, then know that it is time-consuming. You will have to spend time cooking and this is where it can get boring at times. Sometimes, thinking alone of what to cook can be a challenging mountain to climb. This is where having a meal plan helps a lot. Once your meal is planned out, you will just go straight ahead to cook your food and save yourself the time you waste on thinking what am I to cook.

The good thing about the Ketogenic diet is that you do not need to count the calories that you take per meal. However, for those who still want to know the exact amount of nutrient that they are consuming, a prepared meal plan is just the right thing you need. With your meal plan, you are able to know what exactly to eat and the amount of calorie content in each diet.

How to Enter Ketosis Fast

There are practical ways to ensure that you enter into ketosis within a short time. It is only when you do this that you will enter into ketosis within a short time. It all depends on how fast you want to get into ketosis. Below are some of the things that you can do in order to ensure that ketosis mode is activated.

- **Reduce Carb Intake**: to achieve ketosis, you need to restrict the amount of carbohydrate that you consume to 20 grams per day. The intake of 20 grams per day is the recommended amount of carbs that you need for fully optimized ketosis and effective Ketogenic diet. However, you need to understand that the lesser carb you absorb into your system, the quicker your ketosis. It is important for you to understand that your ketosis activation is strictly in your hands. Always remember that the lesser the amount of carbs that you intake, the faster you get into ketosis.

- **Reduce Protein Intake**: Before you enter into Ketosis, one thing you need to know is that you will have to keep an eye on your protein intake. It should never be above 50 grams to 100 grams for ladies and for men, it should be about 70 grams of protein daily. If you ingest that amount of protein and found out that after some days, you have not still entered into ketosis, then you will have to cut it further down. Why do you need to keep an eye on your protein intake? Now, if you consume excess protein than what your body requires, the body converts this protein into glucose. This will hinder you from getting into ketosis because you have glucose in your body and the organs will rather make use of it than embark on using fat as a fuel source. It is only when glucose intake is restricted whether through protein converted to glucose or through carbs that you will enter ketosis fully. The ball is in your hands and you can kick it however you desire.

- **Increase Fat Intake**: to have an effective ketosis within the shortest possible time, fat must constitute at least above 70 percent of your calories. Eat more of Hollandaise, Avocado, egg yolk, olives, meat, pork, etc. You can also get fat from this variety of products:

1. Chicken fat

2. Coconut oil

3. Grass-fed butter

4. Peanut oil

5. Grass fed beef tallow

6. Lard gotten from pigs

7. Organic and pastured chicken Eggs

8. Palm oil

- **Watch your Snack Intake**: Too much of snack can hinder you from entering into full ketosis within the shortest time.

- **Irregular Fasting**: The attainment of ketosis is something you must learn to build up with time. In some other situations, fasting will help you to enter into ketosis faster. This is something you must do by yourself. When you have achieved full ketosis status, then this becomes the natural thing that will be happening to you. This is because as you get into full ketosis, you will experience a steady and a washing away of your desire to eat. What do I mean? It means that when you have entered into ketosis on a Ketogenic diet, you will notice a reduction of your appetite. The occurrence of this may take time, but it will surely happen. Skipping a breakfast or dinner will be of immense help as it will hasten your entrance into the door of ketosis.

- **Forming Good Habit**: Achieving ketosis within the shortest time is easy but impossible without the development of good habit pattern. Without discipline, it is impossible to achieve full blown ketosis status. Sometimes, you will be magnetized by your regular carb diet. They may sometimes be too tempting to resist and it will want to oppose Ketogenic diet and close the gate of ketosis from opening to you. You know the rules, eat your daily 20 grams of carb per day and your high fat of 70 to 80 percent. Your protein intake should be about 70 grams or lesser not more than that. It is a discipline which you have to learn. When the desire for high carb diet is burning intensely in you, the first thing to do is to ensure that you eat some nuts especially those that are very low in carbs like walnut. It is this habit that if well-formed will help you in entering ketosis in time and maintain that state.

Beyond doubt, the reservoir of knowledge that you have has been increased as it regards Ketogenic diet. If we stop at this point, it will be a dwarf understanding of Ketogenic diet. We have made huge progress so far since beginning this book and it seems that one important thing has not been discussed yet. It is therefore highly imperative that we further this knowledge. We will be discussing something that is fundamental. Before you enter into a full ketosis mode, your body like a computer is initializing. It is taking some important steps towards entering into ketosis. Please permit my use of language in making reference to a computer. However, when full ketosis mode is activated, what are the reactions that you will experience within your body. It is this body reaction to a Ketogenic diet that many categorize as the disadvantages of Ketogenic diet. How do you also measure ketosis? We will be paying attention to some of these reactions and measurement of ketosis.

For the purposes of emphasis, the Ketogenic diet plan is more effective when your body gets into ketosis where your body switches from a carb burning machine to a fat burning machine. As this happens, the end products that are generated are called ketones. These ketones come out through the breath when it takes on a fruity dimension, urine, and even sweat. In effect, by testing your urine it is possible to know whether you are in ketosis. The question is how do I measure my ketones level? I will say here that if you desire to measure it, it is a matter of set goals. You should not allow measuring ketones to become your primary consuming passion. You will get into ketosis and you will lose weight, but do not pay too much attention to it so that you will begin to worry much.

Common Challenges of Ketogenic dieters

The Ketogenic diet has come under severe attack in the recent years with many saying that there is no scientific basis for the diet. Nevertheless, I have given you the scientific proof of the diet in this book. Beyond that, many people have had success stories from this diet from weight loss to a healthy life. The diet has its own challenges. There are difficulties and challenges that you will experience. It may be different but they are challenges that you can triumph.

Products Labels

Although I have suggested buying all of your products directly from the farmers market near you for effective Ketogenic diet, there are certain circumstances that will require you buying from the store. This is to ensure that what you are buying is organic. If you have to buy anything that is organic from the store, then make sure that you read every label carefully. I suggest making a thorough check of your item to find the best Ketogenic diet product. Buying your veggies and other stuff from the farmers market near you is the best thing that can happen to you. However, where you cannot buy directly from the farmers market near your area, make sure that you check the product's label very carefully. If you do not do this, it is possible to buy foods that are high in carb content.

Indecision

Sometimes your body might want to tempt you into the state of unpreparedness. It may want to keep you in a permanent cycle of indecision, "I will soon begin my diet." The word soon keeps happening to you until it gets to a point when you will lose complete and total interest in the diet. Never wait for the perfect time for you to start your Ketogenic diet. It is possible to feel completely unprepared for the necessary change. Some people are stuck in an everlasting chain of research. "I need to know this before I begin my diet." Don't get stuck in that. Change is something that is not comfortable to make and if you keep searching for excuses, then it is possible not to begin the diet at all.

Diet Apathy

The ketogenic diet is indeed a fun-filled from the beginning to the end. Will this remain so until the end? If you log onto any of the social media, be it Instagram, Twitter, or even Facebook, you will be over flooded with people's good days that gives you a perfect interest about the diet. Nevertheless, the bad days are coming and when they come, you have to learn to make it exciting. The veterans in the diet have their bad days when Ketogenic diet food becomes boring. During that time, the temptation to return to the old fashion of eating is usually strong. Do not let these feelings take control of you. Rather, you should control them. Sometimes the feelings of resentment, frustration, tiredness, with cooking becoming a chore. When you experience these times, know that it is normal. It happens. Acknowledge this and give yourself space to feel it, and try to get over it. I recommend strongly having a meal plan so that you can have different things to eat on different days. It adds interest and kills apathy. At such times, you can also seek the advice of other dieters on how they overcame their bad days. Belong to a forum and join a community of Ketogenic dieters. It will help you in the days of diet struggles.

Strange Reactions

The moment you change your normal diet to a Ketogenic diet, some persons in your life will begin to express their own insecurities and fears through the comments they that will make on your diet. They will not stop there but will go ahead and make more comments if you lose more weight. Many will tell you how they can never give up their carb foods. Should that border you? No. You have chosen the path of healthy eating, be proud to walk through it. The opinion of people and what they think should not hinder you. Just know that not everybody will be comfortable with the way that you eat. That is the reason why you should be meticulous with people who are your friends. Many of them might discourage you. People who will understand and reason with you can be a great source of encouragement to you.

CHAPTER FOUR

Shopping Tips for Ketogenic Diet

You have read how to do a low dollar Ketogenic diet, but unless you know some shopping tips, it is possible to spend more on your diet making it uncomfortable for you to continue dieting. Shopping! With its many beautiful and eye, magnetizing shelves that are loaded with goods can become the place where you spend a lot of money. For Ketogenic dietary purposes, always buy food items from the farmers market near you.

Shop for Mostly Organic Foods

Foods in their natural state are the best for Ketogenic diet. Many of the foods that have been refined have had their nutrients washed away through the process of refinement. They mostly lack the essential nutrients that you need. Shop wisely.

Follow the Principles of Time

The best time to shop as I have recommended in the low dollar Ketogenic diet is to do it after evening meals. However, you have to strike a balance between evening meals and rush hour. This is because rushing up to purchase things could make you miss the important details on labels of food products. If you rush, chances are that you may not read products label well. It may read "zero carbs" or "carb free" but it contains carb. Besides, if it is rush hour shopping, the queues are normally longer. Frustration can build. Grocery shopping is an important thing that you need some level of focus to do effectively. This is because what you are buying can affect your health and the health of your family too. If it can affect them, then it is something you should not rush.

Carefully Study Your Shopping Aisle

Some of the aisles where you see cheap products might have some of the healthiest foods. So do not ignore them. Arm yourself with a shopping list and thoroughly search them. Do not overlook them because they can give you some healthy foods that you need.

Study Carefully the Ingredients Details

It is fundamental for effective shopping to read the ingredients that are contained in a product that you want to buy. If the ingredient contains what will hinder your Ketogenic diet, then put it down. If you buy ingredients that are high in carb, then you are likely not to lose weight rapidly.

Small Cart for Cutting Expenses

Except if you are going for a bulk purchase or you are using a coupon, it is wise to pick a small cart or basket that is available to you. Why do you need to do that? This will help you make wise purchases. The smaller the cart, the fewer items that you are likely to purchase. However, if you decide to pick up a trolley and glide it across different aisles, I can assure you that you are likely to purchase products for your Ketogenic diet, which you have at home.

Refrigerated Products

Some of the veggies that you will purchase may be frozen. Does that mean that they are bad? No. These veggies are still as nutritious as the fresh ones. The Jerusalem artichokes, carrots and brussels sprouts are still fresh and important even though they may look frozen.

Pay Cash

You may be thinking that buying your products on credits is more efficient for your shopping. Many people who go to the grocery store to buy food products purchase more junk and processed foods. So unless you are short of cash, buy the product and pay in cash. In addition, if you want to buy on credit, then do not buy junk food. If you buy junk and processed foods; your rapid weight loss will not be achieved.

Change Your Shopping Time

This is sound wisdom. Many Americans prefer shopping on Saturdays and Sundays. During those weekends, where most people are not busy, the grocery store is filled with people. Avoid that. This is the attitude of most Americans. You can change your shopping time to Tuesday if you are free or Fridays. Depending on how relaxed your schedules are. Then your Saturdays will be for cooking your diet meals. I have said it that if you want to cut down the cost of your Ketogenic diet, then you must learn to prepare everything by yourself. Beyond that, for people with children who are employed, you can use your weekend to prepare your meals and refrigerate them. Then from Monday to Fridays, you put your foods in a bag and head to your job. Just make sure that you cook different foods during the weekend so that you do not get bored with eating the same meal.

Watch Out For Fancy Labels

Have you realized that products that are more expensive come in fancy packages? A study has found that food suppliers employ the use of fancy fonts and labels as an excuse for their high price. The research had further stated that people tend to think that they will get more value for their money from fancy and attractive product labels.

Avoid Prepared Food Sections

Have you seen the prepared food sections of many grocery stores in the country? It has experienced tremendous growth in recent years because many in America are looking for alternatives to expensive restaurants. In 2011, the supermarket restaurants in the USA grew to 14 billion dollars. Why? Because many Americans are looking for alternatives to the lower cost of food. However, you need to understand that if you want to lower the cost of your Ketogenic diet, you must make a conscious effort to go for your shopping alone and avoid eating in the supermarket restaurants. Now combine this tip with low dollar Ketogenic diet and you will cut the cost of dieting to the lowest form.

Buy Unpopular Brand

Stay on the shelf or die! Many big manufacturers in America are using all forms of malpractices to keep small manufacturers out of the shelf. Independent Marketers in California sued Sara Lee for paying supermarkets so that their products are at the bottom of the shelf. However, some of this unknown brand have the healthiest foods than the famous brands.

Low Dollar Ketogenic diet

Many people starting out the Ketogenic diet are not aware of how expensive it is. Until they begin the diet and realize that, their bills increased ten times over. That is when they will begin to complain that the diet is too expensive and they cannot continue with it. For best Ketogenic diet, most of your foods will be organic. In the grocery store, some of the most expensive food products in the store are organic foods. This, therefore, means that anyone who wants to do the Ketogenic diet must be ready to spend money on his diet. However, I will tell you how you can be on the diet and still spend a little amount of money.

Prioritization

This is the first place to begin your Ketogenic diet. You have to make a decision on what is more important. The Ketogenic diet lifestyle requires this decision. There are certain things that are not important that steadily drain down dollars from your wallet. I will leave that decision to you. Nevertheless, what if the money spent on some of the pleasurable things in your life can be given up and devoted to your diet? Setting your priorities right is important. Spend money on things that are important to you. Your pleasurable sports can be limited to feed your Ketogenic diet bill. If the things that are in your life right now are things of necessity, then that is good and excellent. Many people are murmuring about the expensiveness of the Ketogenic diet, however, they have many fancy things that pile up bills. A life lived in health when the money is spent on this diet by far outweighs being an ever present guest in a hospital or even buying expensive health care insurance. The food you eat has a direct link to your health.

Avoid Waste

Let nothing be wasted! It will help you to cut down cost. This is the most efficient way to manage resources. For instance, the bones you have used are not to be discarded; you can reuse them for making another set of broth. The pan drippings you have used can be reserved for future usage. For your fresh produce, employ wisdom. Do not waste it. Cut just about what you need. Throw nothing away.

This is the biggest problem of dieters – whether they are veteran dieters or beginners. Food wastage will draw many holes in your wallet and finances. Your leftovers should not be a bosom friend of the dustbin. It should be frozen in the refrigerator to be used again. A food saver will help you to save money. Your vegetables may not look freshly appetizing from 3 days ago but they are still delicious with a nutritional value. So don't waste any of your food. It will make your low dollar Ketogenic diet a reality.

Direct Farmers Purchase

The farmers market that is near you is a great source of fresh and inexpensive food. Once you identify yourself with the local farmers around you, it will amaze you the amount of money that you will save when you have a personal relationship with the local farmers and you begin to buy fresh produce directly from them. As you devote your loyalty to them by making regular purchases, they will give you items like bones and organs at a discount. Besides that, after a hot farming day, many farmers are constrained by situations to sell their farm produce so that it does not waste. The farmers may be willing to sell their produce at a cheaper rate.

Buy Food Items Nearing Expiring Date

The best time to go for grocery shopping is just before your evening meal. Meats and items that are nearing their expiry date are heavily discounted. Do not be alarmed, they are good for consumption.

Buy In Bulk

One of the easiest ways to save money is to purchase your food items in bulk. For instance, a bag of chicken in a nearby store around you can be $ 10 and can last you almost a week. For those who want to shop online, check for Grassland Beef that can be shipped to your house in a frozen box. The great thing about bulk buying is that it gives a discount that you will not be able to get if you buy your items one after the other. If the goods that you want to purchase are seasonal goods, then during the season make your purchases in large quantity. If you buy in bulk, you can preserve the freshness of your product by either freezing, fermenting or other methods of preservation that is best suited to you.

Personally make your stuff

If you buy everything you need for your Ketogenic diet, it will increase your expenses. However, if make your own flavor, your spending on the diet will be little. Prepare your homemade stock and other condiments that you make by yourself. This will reduce expenses. Let this be a discipline that you will learn every time by making your own stuff from the scratch. What you need if you want to make everything yourself are the basic ingredients.

Effective Budget Planning

When you plan a budget, it will help you to keep an eye on what, where and which things are needed to be purchased. It will empower you to keep away from ostentatious purchases that pile up the mountains and the hills of bills. Expensive snacks and desserts that increase your spending should be avoided through effective budget planning.

Adopt Simple Meal Plans

Keep everything simple. Prepare most of your meals using cheap items for your diet. The simpler the better as this will cut down your spending a lot.

Cultivate a Garden

For those who love gardening, you have an added advantage towards lowering the cost of your Ketogenic diet meals. With a tiny amount of $2 invested in each plant, it will surprise you at a number of plants that you will produce from your homemade garden. Thinking of how to begin, all you need is a windowsill for your herb garden which will give you fresh herbs from your home directly.

Plan Ahead

To be successful in your Ketogenic diet by lowering cost, then planning is your number one key. If you plan your meals ahead of time, you will reduce cost. It all depends on your personal preference and style. While others can cook food from available ingredients, yet for some, they need planning in order to be effective. So style your cooking according to what you know that you can do. Planning for some people is an indispensable tool while others need not make a plan to avoid wastage. It is possible that your plan may change from one day to another. To preserve your own food, it is highly important that the leftovers food that has a short lifespan such as berries and vegetables are eaten within few days after consumption.

Costco Membership

Aimed at cutting down the cost of your Ketogenic diet, then you may consider Costco membership or any membership at your local food store or market. Although I will always suggest buying all your Ketogenic diet recipes directly from the farmers market available near you. Does that mean that those who are not able to buy directly from the farmers market cannot do the Ketogenic diet? The answer is no. If you can't buy directly from the market, then I will suggest getting a Costco membership card. The membership card for gold card owners will cost you an amazing $ 55 per year. There is another membership card that cost $ 110 per year. Depending on your financial weight, you can get a membership card and enjoy a lot of discounts. A complete rotisserie chicken will cost you $ 5 and they are very big and two dozen of eggs cost just $ 3. There are other inexpensive items when purchased in bulk such as oils, nuts, avocado, meat, and cheese. You can also buy your items at Costco in bulk. This will help you to save a lot of money and cut down the cost of your Ketogenic diet. If you live in the UK, Costco in London is three – Chingford, Thurrock, and Wardford. If you live in Germany, you can find Costco in Berlin, Frankfurt, and Hussen. In Australia, you can find Costco in Docklands, Canberra, Auburn, and Adelaide. Besides that, you can do a simple Google search of Costco near you.

Coupons, Gifts, and Discounts

There are many coupons for your Ketogenic diet food items in many grocery stores around you. If you decide to use them, you will reduce the cost of your diet. With the abundance of android apps, many of them can give you coupons that you can use for purchasing keto food items. Many stores are willing to offer you a reward for your loyalty with a coupon or a membership card. With your membership card, you can get special offers for food items and in some cases home delivery services. Even online stores offer coupons. You can use them to make your purchases and get discounts.

Use a Dehydrator

The use of a refrigerator is a great idea for the preservation of food items. However, beyond the use of a refrigerator, a dehydrator can be used to preserve your food items. Sometimes, the store offers more for sale than the space in your refrigerator. You may want to use the opportunity to buy more meat since they are sold at a discount price. Dehydrate the meat and store it for future use. If you have a garden and your garden produces a lot of foods than you need, your refrigerator being full, your dehydrator can be used to preserve the foods that can be used in the future.

Purchase during Seasonal Availability

Veggies from the farmers market are seasonal. This means that there are times when they will be cheaper because it is their seasons. Although this will never be the case for you if you make your purchases from the stores. You will only notice it when it is not the season in their price. It will be slightly more expensive when it is the beginning of their seasons since it is not available in large quantity. Due to increased growth of technology and the prevalence of preservation machinery, stores around the world can offer food items at any time of the year. It is not uncommon to see fresh strawberries in the month of February or even pumpkin during the month of June on the shelves of many grocery stores, but because it is the store and you make these purchases at your convenience, it will cost you more.

Search for Cheaper Suppliers near You

You may want to make a list of suppliers whose products and services are cheaper in your location. This will help you to cut down the cost of your Ketogenic diet. Categorize your suppliers. Know those whose meat and animal products are cheaper, your baking essentials, veggies and fruits, sweeteners, nuts and seeds, berries and spices. Find out those who offer the cheaper sale of eggs, fruits, and chicken. If you are in Canada or UK or Germany or Australia, you can take your search to the internet and look for the available store that sells cheap stuff.

It will help you to cut down the cost of your Ketogenic diet.

Prepare a Shopping List

Thinking of hitting the road to the store for shopping, always prepare a shopping list. Have a piece of paper or an iPad or android apps for your shopping list preparation. The advantage of this is to ensure that you know exactly what you want to purchase so that you do not go and buy things you might not need.

Buy Inexpensive Ketogenic Diet Recipes

Have you seen the price of organic recipes in the store? Expensive huh? Yes, they are and to lower the cost of your Ketogenic diet, buy inexpensive recipes. Buy simple recipes like meat, seasonal veggies, nuts, and cheese.

Purchase Cheaper Meat Cut

There are many cheaper types of meat cut out there. For effective cooking of meat cuts, make use of a pressure cooker or slow cooker. It will cook the meat for you so that it can fall apart. Marrow bones and offal with their high nutrient contents are usually cheaper than other cuts.

Know What Beef to Buy

Grass-fed or pastured or grain-fed beef? Which of these will cut down the cost of your Ketogenic diet? Grass fed animals are those animals that have been feeding on grass for their whole life. Can animals that fed grass and during winter silage be called grass fed? No. They are not. They are rather pastured-fed animals. Grain fed meat from animals that have been in confinement should be avoided. However, buy the one that you can afford to purchase employing all the methods discussed above for lowering the cost of your purchases.

Eat Dessert Occasionally

Ketogenic diet desserts are many. The Desserts may look so wonderful but it may add to the expenses of your diet. It is sound wisdom to eat dessert occasionally in order to cut down the cost of your diet. Though delicious, the more treats you eat, the more expensive your diet will be. To cut costs, these desserts should be eaten infrequently and should not be daily affairs except you do not want to live the low the dollar Ketogenic diet lifestyle.

CHAPTER FIVE

Introduction

One of the reasons why the Ketogenic diet has gained a lot of acceptance today is because of its ability to help many dieters achieve quick and a rapid weight loss. Where other forms of diet have failed, the Ketogenic diet has triumphed. That is why it has achieved many laurels of successes as seen in the acceptance that it has obtained so far even among dietitians, physicians, and dieters. By restricting the intake of carbs which end product is glucose, you set yourself on a course of having your body change from burning glucose as energy to burning fat. This change in body usage of fuel comes when the dieter enters into ketosis. It is during ketosis that ketone bodies are produced due to the body consistent breakdown of stored fat. Having stated that, does Ketogenic diet has any therapeutic benefit? Many researchers in recent years have surfaced showing that Ketogenic diet can be used to cure multiple diseases. If you recalled, one of the main reasons why this diet gathered a lot of acceptance in the society today is its cure or regulation of epilepsy. But today, it has extended its frontiers from epilepsy to many other therapeutic remedies. Beyond this, it is important to highlight some of the withdrawal symptoms likely to be encountered when a dieter decides to stop the Ketogenic diet. Why am I doing that? I do not want you to begin to worry thinking that something has happened to your health. Let us now look at some of the medical benefits of Ketogenic diet which dieters are more likely to benefit from.

Medical Effects of Ketogenic Diet

A lot of scientific research has been conducted that have discovered a lot of elements in Ketogenic diets with varied therapeutic benefits. I will make a list of them for you. Here they are:

- Epilepsy
- Alzheimer Disease
- Parkinson Disease
- Cancer
- Diabetes
- Autism
- Migraine

- Acne
- Reduction of blood sugar and insulin
- Reduce blood pressure
- Cure for many brain disorders
- Anti-aging
- Amyotrophic Lateral Sclerosis
- Stroke
- Cure for Mitochondrial Disorder
- Cure for Brain Trauma

From the above list, it can be seen that the health benefits of Ketogenic diet are numerous. Do you know anyone or family members suffering from the above-listed diseases, then your solution lies in this diet. Put them on it and see a remarkable improvement in their health status.

Withdrawal Symptoms of Ketogenic Diet

Many Ketogenic diet books will never tell you this because they are trying to sell their books to you and make sure that you buy it. But I have decided that beyond selling this book to you, I am giving you a much vital information that will help you anytime you decided to put a pause on the Ketogenic diet for a while. The burning question is, what will happen when you eventually stop the Ketogenic diet and returned back to your normal diet or change to other forms of low carb diets?

We will consider some of these factors and I will tell you what you can do to still be able to maintain your weight after stopping the Ketogenic diet.

- **Weight Gain**: We have stated somewhere in this book that Ketogenic diet is a fast weight loss diet that enables dieters to lose weight with unimaginable speed. While this is true and an established fact, there are many things that will happen to you once you want to withdraw from the Ketogenic diet. One of it is weight gain. You were on a low-carb diet that helped you burnt down fat. However, when you stop the Ketogenic diet, it is possible to gain back all the weight that you have lost. When you stop Keto and you go back to your old eating habit, you will gain back all the weight that you have lost. If you continue eating just the way that you desire, it is possible to even gain more weight than you had before going Ketogenic diet. How then do you overcome that? The first thing to do is to maintain your low-level calorie diet. I told you about habit formation. It is important to develop good habits. Avoid eating processed foods and keep an eye on your carb intake. Once you are able to maintain a good eating habit, you can maintain your weight which you had before you started your Ketogenic diet.

- **Loss of Hair**: It is possible to experience hair loss when you are making a switch from a Ketogenic diet to other diets or from Ketogenic diet to normal diet. This is the experience that many people have because of the big change from Ketogenic diet to other forms of diet. It is a withdrawal symptom that some people tend to report once making a change from Keto to another form of diet. This experience happens when you are brushing your hair. However, this is temporal as once you make the full adjustment by stopping the Ketogenic diet, it will stop with time.

- **Normal Breath**: Most Keto dieters experience a lot of bad breath where their breath takes on a fruity smell. This is the because of the ketones that are escaping through their breath. However, when changing from Keto to other forms of diet or normal diet, you are likely to experience good breath.

- **A Higher level of Energy**: When transitioning from a normal diet to Ketogenic diet, one of the temporal things you will encounter is the lower level of energy that you will experience in your level of endurance. The reason for this is because your body has been used to carbs as a fuel source for many years. However, as you returned back to normal diet, the experience of higher energy and performance is instant because your body is returning back to what it is used to. This is one of the withdrawal symptoms of Ketogenic diet.

- **Adaptable Metabolism**: The human body goes through a lot of adaptive changes as you change from one fuel source to another. One of the withdrawal effects that you will notice is the quick adaptability to the new fuel which is carb. But eat carb wisely and watch your calorie intake else you might end up gaining more weight than you had expected.

- **Revitalize carb craving**: Be careful! One of the withdrawal symptoms that you notice is revitalized carb cravings. You will begin to desire more carbs than you can imagine. Discipline is your key. If you want to maintain your weight, then you will have to fight your craving for carbs.

Body Reaction to Ketogenic Diet

There are certain things that you need to expect when you are switching from either another low carb diet to a Ketogenic diet or from your normal high carb diet to Ketogenic diet. Your body has been used to one type of fuel source which is carb. So when a change is made, there are certain reactions to expect. I will mention them here quickly:

- Poor Mental Focus (happens within 2 -3 days of going Keto, it stops with time.)
- Loss of Strength and Endurance Ability.
- Bad Breath (to stop this, drink much salt and water, brush teeth frequently)
- Irregular heart beats (drink more liquid and salt to stop this)
- Reduced Physical Performance.
- Constipation (mostly for beginners, drink enough water, salt and liquid, and veggies).
- Dehydration (mostly for beginners, drink plenty liquid).
- Muscle Cramps.
- Flu.

CHAPTER SIX

Introduction

We will consider something else for the purposes of effective Ketogenic diet – exercise as a way of furthering your Ketogenic diet. What type of exercise do you need to do that will ensure faster weight loss? We will look at them very briefly.

In the past, there were so many misconceptions about being on a Ketogenic diet and engaging in different forms of exercise. This form of misconception and propaganda has been set in motion by the conjectures flown around on the internet and many research studies. Many of the physicians who fought against being on a Ketogenic diet and engaging in thorough exercise did so because of the insufficient knowledge which they had. Besides, their information was not evidential neither was it factual but on the basis of inchoate knowledge. But as the medical field became agog with information regarding the diet, with many research being birthed on the diet that experts placed participants on a high carb diet, and those on a Ketogenic diet to test the efficacy of their strength during exercise, it was realized that those on the Ketogenic diet did well with an enduring strength.

To begin with, you are closer to the gate of losing weight more effectively when you are on a Ketogenic diet than those who are not on the diet. The reason for this is because when your body is in Ketosis, every bit and ounce of your energy come from fat. In effect, even when your body is in a state of rest, your stored body fat is still being utilized by your body which in turns makes you look slim fit. But with Ketogenic diet, you get better results from your weight loss program when you attach it to some form of exercise. This is very vital please pay attention. For people who are on a high carb diet, they have to exercise for a long period of time for them to enter into their fat burning point. It may take probably about twenty or more minutes to reach the point of burning fat. On the converse, for people or persons who are on a Ketogenic diet, they are constantly at the state or point of burning fat once ketosis has been attained, hence the potential of your weight loss during a workout is higher. When you decide to work out, you add more lean body muscle that increases the rate of burning energy than when you decide not to work out. The fundamental difference between Keto dieters one on a workout and the other not on a workout program are the ratios of weight loss. While the one on workout loses weight faster, the other one who is not on a workout loses weight at a slower rate compared to the one who is steadily taking in dosages of exercises. It is highly recommended if you want to lose weight faster to adopt an exercise plan that is different from your diet plan. It is essential to know that if you have not been exercising and want to begin one during a Ketogenic diet, it should be done slowly and with time you can increase your workout. Thirty minutes per day of easy cardio will be sufficient. Exercises like – walking, swimming, and resistance training for the purposes of enhancing muscle leanness are good. As your body adapts to regular exercise, you can increase the amount of your workout per day.

Types of Ketogenic Diet for Effective Exercise

As a result of the change in your diet, especially if you are fit and have been exercising regularly, it is possible to feel the absence of glycogen in your muscles. If you are already quite fit and exercise regularly, you may find that the absence of glycogen in your muscles which may sometimes make it difficult for you to be effective in your exercise. Where you find yourself in any of the above-mentioned situations, then the recommendations in this small subhead will be of a pertinent importance to you. For effective exercise tips, it may be possible to attempt a switch from your normal Keto diet to targeted or cyclical Ketogenic diet. We will go ahead to explain these two forms of exercise plan for your Ketogenic diet.

The burning question is, what is a cyclical Ketogenic diet? By definition, a cyclical Ketogenic diet is a standardized procedure for a Ketogenic diet where a person during the week, from Monday to Friday maintains his Ketogenic menu plan strictly but on weekends the amount of carb is increased. In this type of diet plan, the carb load on weekdays is normal while on the weekend, the carb load rate is higher. When you are on a cyclical Ketogenic Diet plan, you will follow a normal diet plan in the course of the week but at weekends, your diet plan takes a slightly higher amount of carb. When you load carbs this way, it will enable you to store some carb energy for the week so that you can have some level of energy for effective workouts. The only days that you will cut down your carb is Monday to Friday while on Saturday and Sunday, you increase the amount of carb intake. In this diet plan, your first 14 days will be the inducement stage where you essentially stick to a low carb Ketogenic diet plan in order for you to go into full blown ketosis. Once you have achieved ketosis, then you can then follow your cyclical Ketogenic diet plan. However, a different plan might work for you.

The Targeted Ketogenic diet plan. Let us make an attempt at explaining what it means. A targeted Ketogenic diet plan means eating more amount of carbs before workouts. In other words, in this type of diet plan, a person will adopt a low carb diet, mainly adhering to his Ketogenic diet plan every day of the week but when the days for the exercise or workouts comes, an extra gram of carb is consumed before exercise. The purpose for this is to boost your glucose to have more energy for the exercise. One good thing about this diet plan is that it does not stop your body from returning back to ketosis status when you are through with your exercise. However, as a note of advice, I will caution you a little about following a cyclical or target Ketogenic diet plan. Why? It is very easy to begin to use the excuse of these diet plans and start to consume excess carbs. If you do this, it will easily throw you out of ketosis. When on a cyclical or targeted diet plan, it is good to avoid fructose type of food and consume more foods that are glucose or dextrose based. The reason for this is because fructose will likely interrupt your ketosis status. If you decide on any of the above-mentioned types of diet that you will want to adapt to make your workouts and cardio exercise very efficient, you must avoid these list of foods which have very high fructose content so you do not fall out of ketosis:

1. Carbonated beverage drinks such as soda

2. Pomegranate juice, especially the one that is bottled.

3. Medjool

4. Nectar from mango

5. Carbonated beverage drink such as ginger ale

6. Tamarind Nectar

7. Raisins

8. Applesauce

9. Ketchup

10. Agave

11. Cranberry juice

12. Cherries

13. Persimmons

14. Vinegar

15. Asparagus

16. Dates

It is important to watch out for these types of food when you have decided that you want to undertake a cyclical or targeted Ketogenic diet. Most of the carbonated beverage drinks have very high level of fructose chief among them sodas like coca-cola, Pepsi, mountain dew, etc these companies use high fructose corn syrup in their products giving it an unlikely high sweetness. Instead of these types of foods, eat foods that are rich in glucose for either of these diets that you have undertaken. Foods like:

- Grains
- Cereal
- Veggies
- Some Nuts and Seeds
- Leguminous foods
- Honey
- Breakfast cereals

General Advice Tips

From the beginning of this book down to the end of it, it is information-packed. We started from the early stage by telling you how the ketone diet came about. However, let me add more value to what your money purchased. I want to give you some general advice tips that will help the course of your weight loss plan.

Planning

Your meals should always be planned ahead of time. The 21-day meal plan outline here is more than silver and gold to help you in your speedy weight loss goals. It is good to think about what you will eat the next day. Always be on the top of your Ketogenic diet game all the time. If during the previous day you have leftovers, make use of them. Do not throw them away. The importance of planning ahead can never be overstated. If during the course of your planning you discovered that there are mistakes in what you are supposed to eat, it is easy to detect them because you have planned ahead. For instance, you can detect if the amount of protein that you are supposed to eat is too high. If the protein is unnecessarily high, it is possible to disturb your ketosis because too much of protein is converted into glucose. Do you see why it is important to plan ahead?

Sleeping and Resting

Sleeping and resting. In recent times, studies have shown that sleep and your appetite are interconnected. This is because your sleep affects the balance of your leptin and ghrelin in the body. Grehlin being a hormone that is produced when a person is hungry, increases your eating appetite. But leptin performs a different function in the body. It is the one that tells the brain that you are full and satisfied so that you don't overeat. Studies have shown that during sleep deprivation leptin level goes down. This decrcase in appetite affects your level of satiation. A study was done by doctors who subjected about 12 persons to 2 days of enough sleep and another set of 2 days of sleep deprivation. It was observed during the research that in the two days of sleeplessness, the level of leptin in the body reduced while the level of ghrelin in the body increased. As a result of this, their appetites increased with a resultant effect on their desire for food and calories which equally experienced a tremendous increase. Another research that tested leptin and Grehlin level and body fat percentage, it revealed that the participants in the study that had less than 8 hours sleep per night experienced increased levels of hormonal activity mainly the ghrelin which instigate the feeling of hunger. I will recommend that if you have insomnia, you should avoid eating your dinner shortly before bedtime. Besides that, always ensure that you have a good sleeping schedule and then cut down on the amount of caffeine in your diet. If you do all of these things and nothing still happens, or you find yourself unable to sleep, darken your room at night before bedtime. You can even resort to the use of a natural supplement to help you find rest at night.

Support Group

Now, like should attract like. It is very good to look for a support group that can help you. There are anti-Ketone dieters everywhere that are not in agreement with the Ketogenic dieters. If you walk in their counsel, rejection will be the very thing that you will experience. It is very important for you to look for support groups around you, fellow ketone dieters that will be willing to assist you and encourage you. If they lose pounds of weight, they come and tell you what they have lost. It is a popular knowledge that many ketone dieters record a higher level of success when they are with a group that supports them. When you are with your support group, you can ventilate or express your grievances and difficulties without being put down. So you have to look for a community of people that are mostly ketone dieters who will not find your diet discomforting and will be willing to support you. This group, of course, will know what your goals are, they will encourage you to pursue them. On the basis of their experiences, these people can help you, assist you in attaining your goals and they can answer your questions too. For beginners, it is possible to experience some things that you could not have read in this Ketogenic diet book. Your support group experience will come in handy to help you in such situations.

Reward Scheme

Encourage yourself and give yourself a medallion of reward. As you achieve the goals that you have set for yourself, you need to reward yourself. I must state here that, rewarding yourself doesn't necessarily mean that you have to eat meals that will endanger your Ketone diet or your Ketosis. You can treat yourself to something nice that doesn't put your Ketogenic diet in danger. You can eat something that is not Ketone inclined but watch it carefully so that you don't put so much effort in your Ketone diet and later it becomes a total and colossal waste. It is ideal to set goals for yourself and when you hit the bar of those goals, give yourself a reward. When you meet the first goal, increase the bar and follow it logically until you smash the next bar. When you do that, reward yourself. If you have to feast on anything during your reward, something like pizza, then ensure it is a low carb. This reward scheme and treating yourself to what you have achieved will keep you highly encouraged. The reward scheme is an encouragement system, built by you to encourage no one but you.

Thank You for purchasing this book. Can you please take a minute and write a review, I appreciate it.

62849540R00051

Made in the USA
Lexington, KY
19 April 2017